S0-AAL-311

*to*

_____

*from*

_____

Live with the objective
of being happy.

—ANNE FRANK

Copyright © 2009 Hallmark Licensing, Inc.

Published by Hallmark Books,
a division of Hallmark Cards, Inc.,
Kansas City, MO 64141
Visit us on the web at www.Hallmark.com.

All rights reserved. No part of this publication may be
reproduced, transmitted, or stored in any form or by any
means without the prior written permission of the publisher.

Editorial Director: Todd Hafer
Editor: Theresa Trinder
Art Director: Kevin Swanson
Designer: Myra Colbert Design
Production Artist: Dan Horton

ISBN: 978-1-59530-034-8

BOK5540

Printed and bound in China

# The SECRETS of SUCCESS

## REALLY SIMPLE RULES
## FOR WHAT REALLY MATTERS

Success. We read books about it, watch infomercials, work really hard to get it, and keep it, and maybe show it off a little.

But what *is* it, exactly?

The world tells us it's getting a good job. Making a lot of money. Driving a new car. It's getting somewhere fast. Knowing someone important. Making something happen. It's being stylish. Being popular. Being in charge.

Or is it something else altogether? Something you can't quite put your finger on. Something almost impossible to describe. Something different for everyone, depending on who you are, where you are, and when.

Poet Matthew Arnold said, "Life is not a having and a getting, but a being and becoming." This is no secret, but it's something we're likely to forget from time to time, especially when the going gets rough, tough, or tiresome. This book has thirty-two such "secrets." Simple rules and reminders. Ways of being and becoming. Ways of sharing yourself with the world.

One thing they say is true: Success is a journey. You are on your way.

You don't have to see
the whole staircase,
just take the first step.

—*Martin Luther King, Jr.*

Believe as many as six impossible things before breakfast.

*—Lewis Carroll*

# SECRET #3

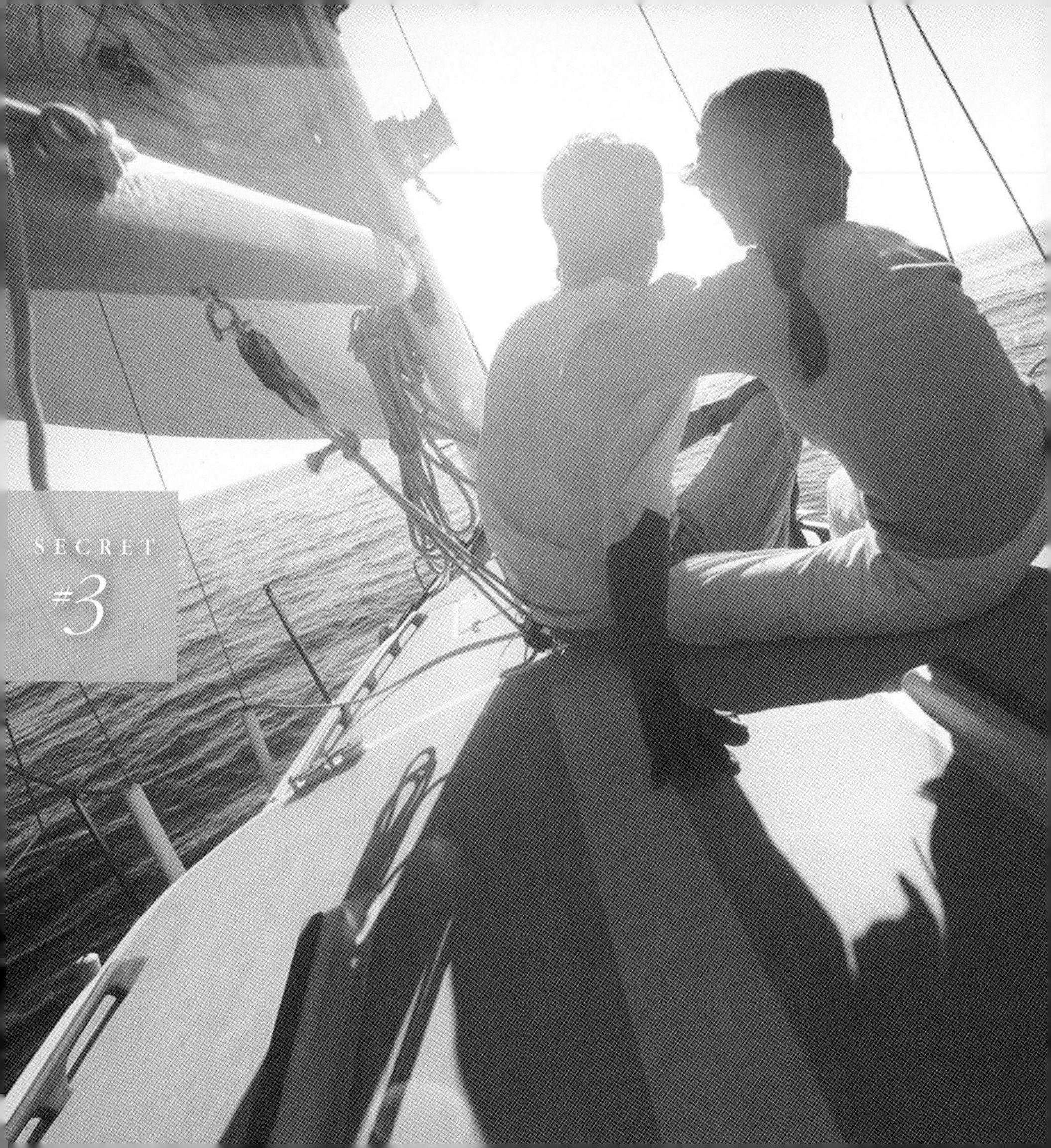

The true delight is in the finding out rather than in the knowing.

—*Isaac Asimov*

Business, you know,
may bring you money,
but friendship
hardly ever does.

—*Jane Austen*

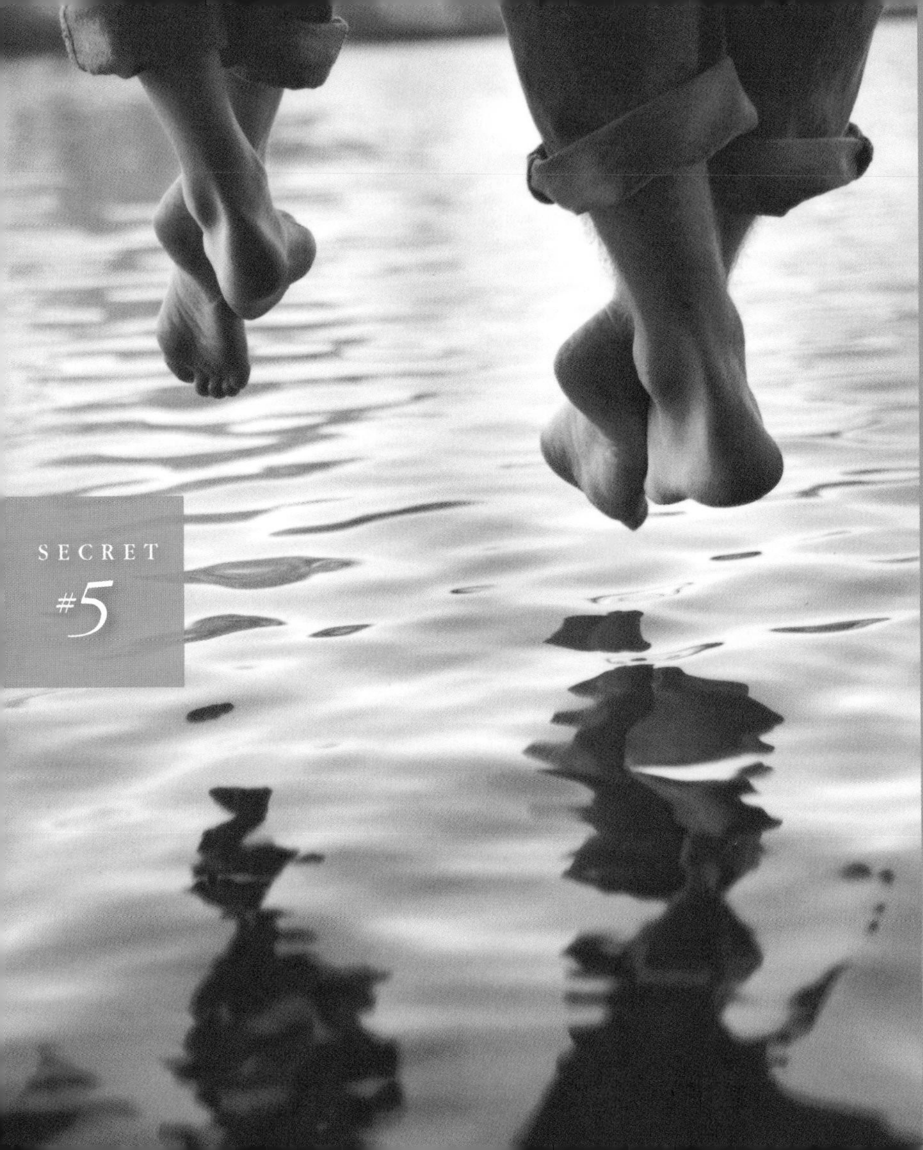

SECRET

#5

How you
spend your
time is more
important than
how you spend
your money.

—*David Norris*

When someone does
something good, applaud!
You will make two people happy.

*—Samuel Goldwyn*

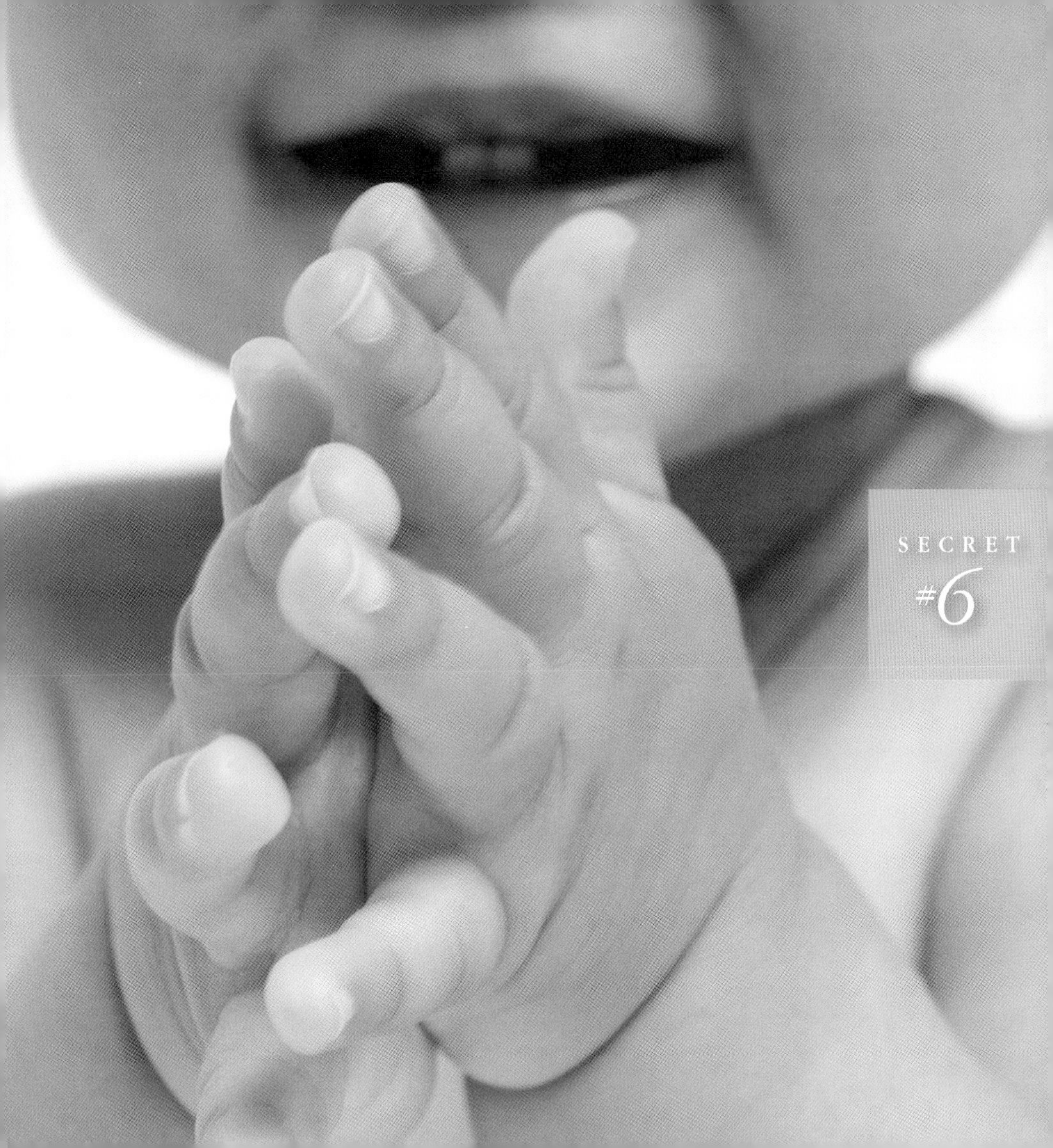

# SECRET #6

SECRET
#7

We all *do re mi,*
but you have got to find
the other notes yourself.

—*Louis Armstrong*

Freedom is not worth having if it does not include the freedom to make mistakes.

—*Mahatma Gandhi*

SECRET
#8

# SECRET #9

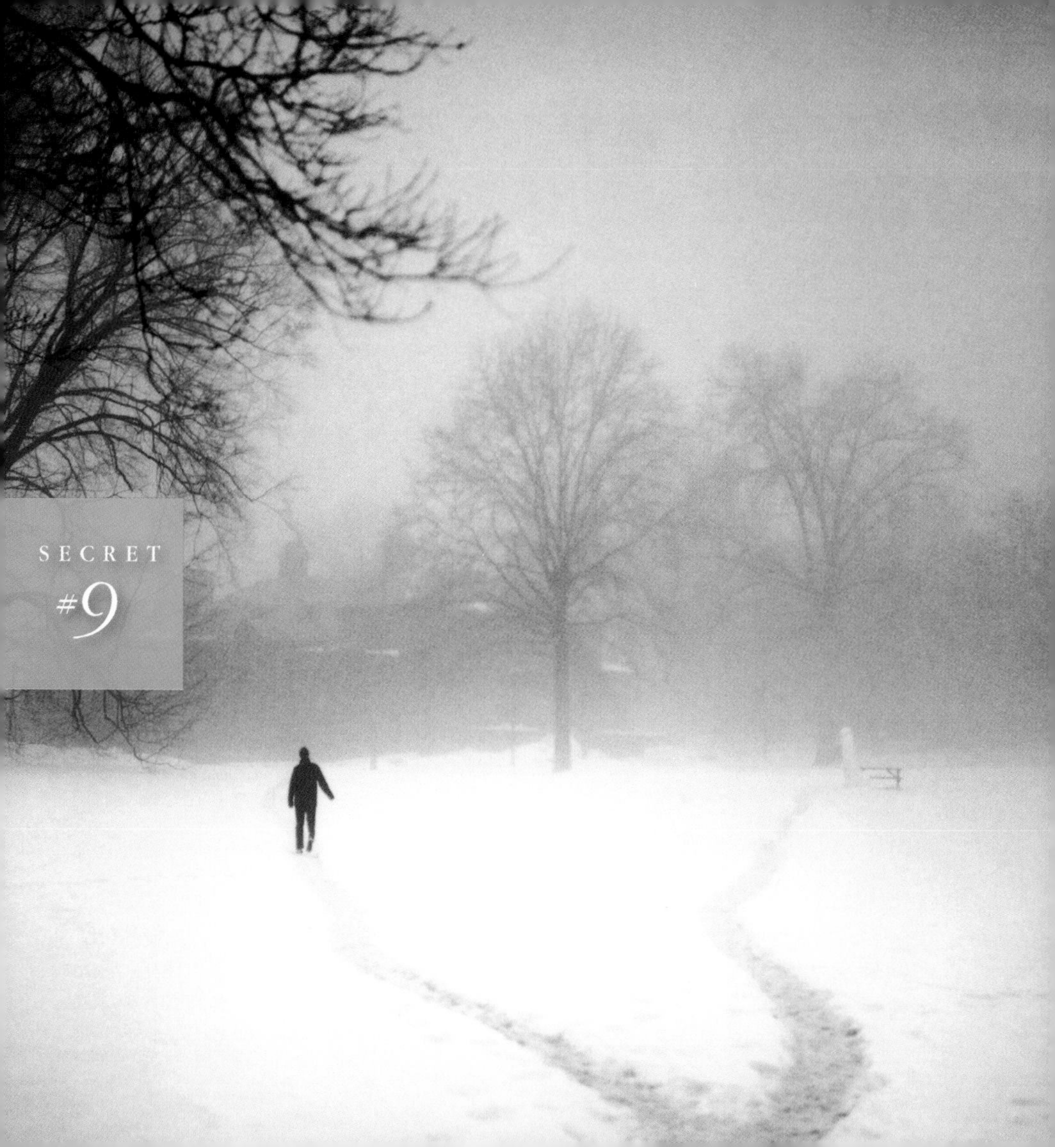

All that is gold
does not glitter;
not all those who
wander are lost.

—*J. R. R. Tolkien*

Our brightest blazes of gladness
are commonly linked by unexpected sparks.

—*Samuel Johnson*

SECRET
#10

SECRET
*#11*

Do what you can
with what you have
where you are.

—*Theodore Roosevelt*

Never be ashamed of tears.

—*Charles Dickens*

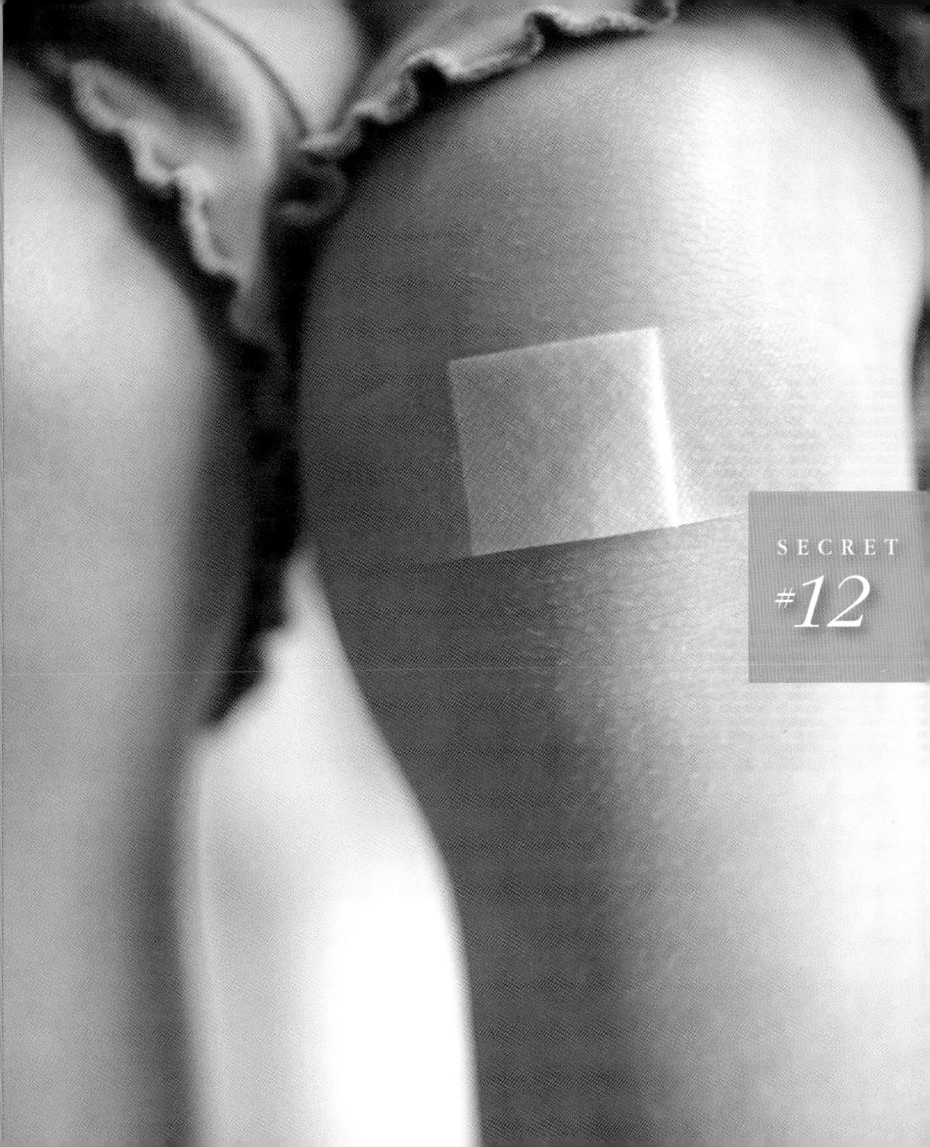

# SECRET #12

# SECRET #13

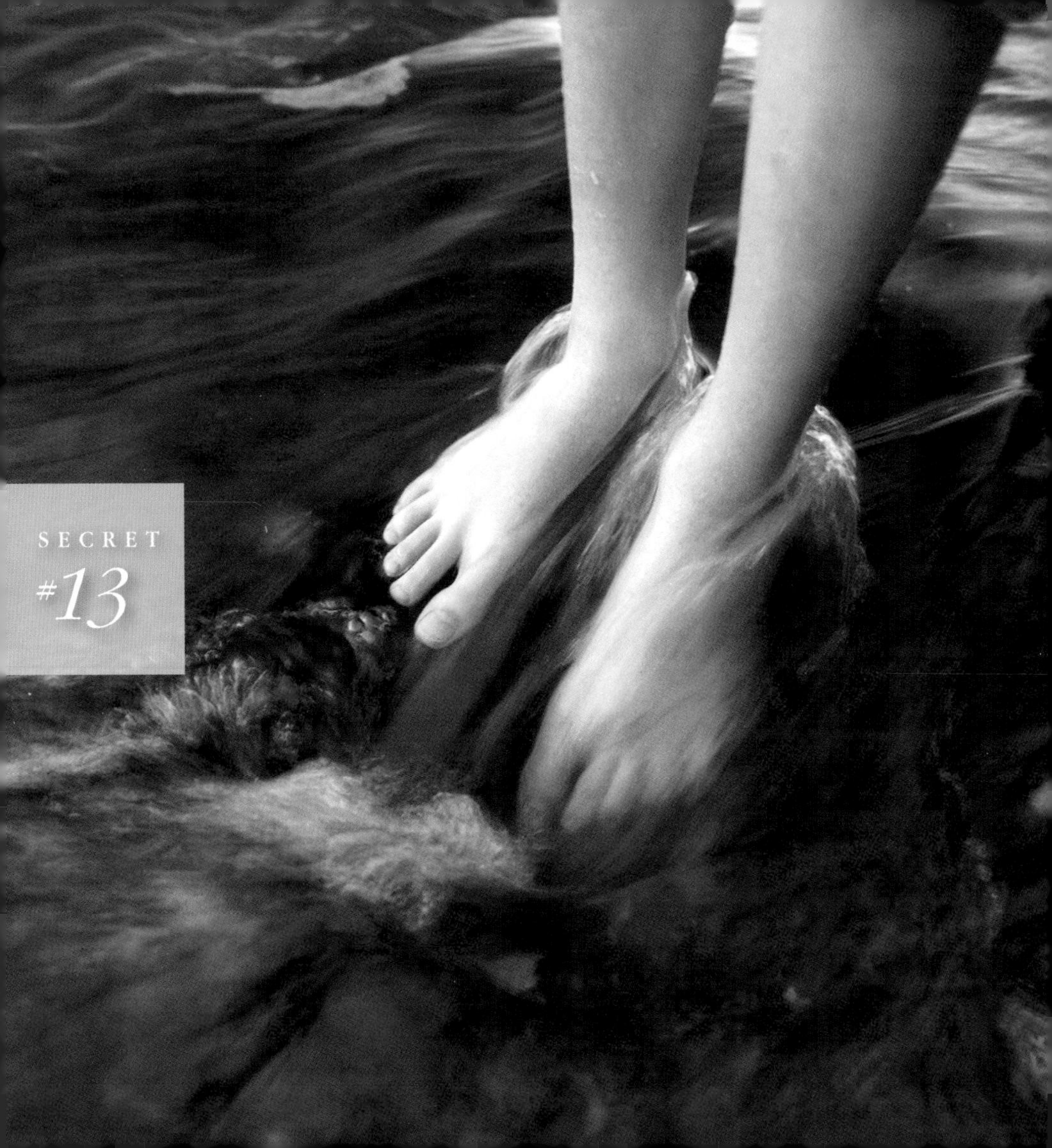

Try to comprehend
a little mystery
every day.

—*Albert Einstein*

Wheresoever you go,
go with all your heart.

—*Confucius*

SECRET
#14

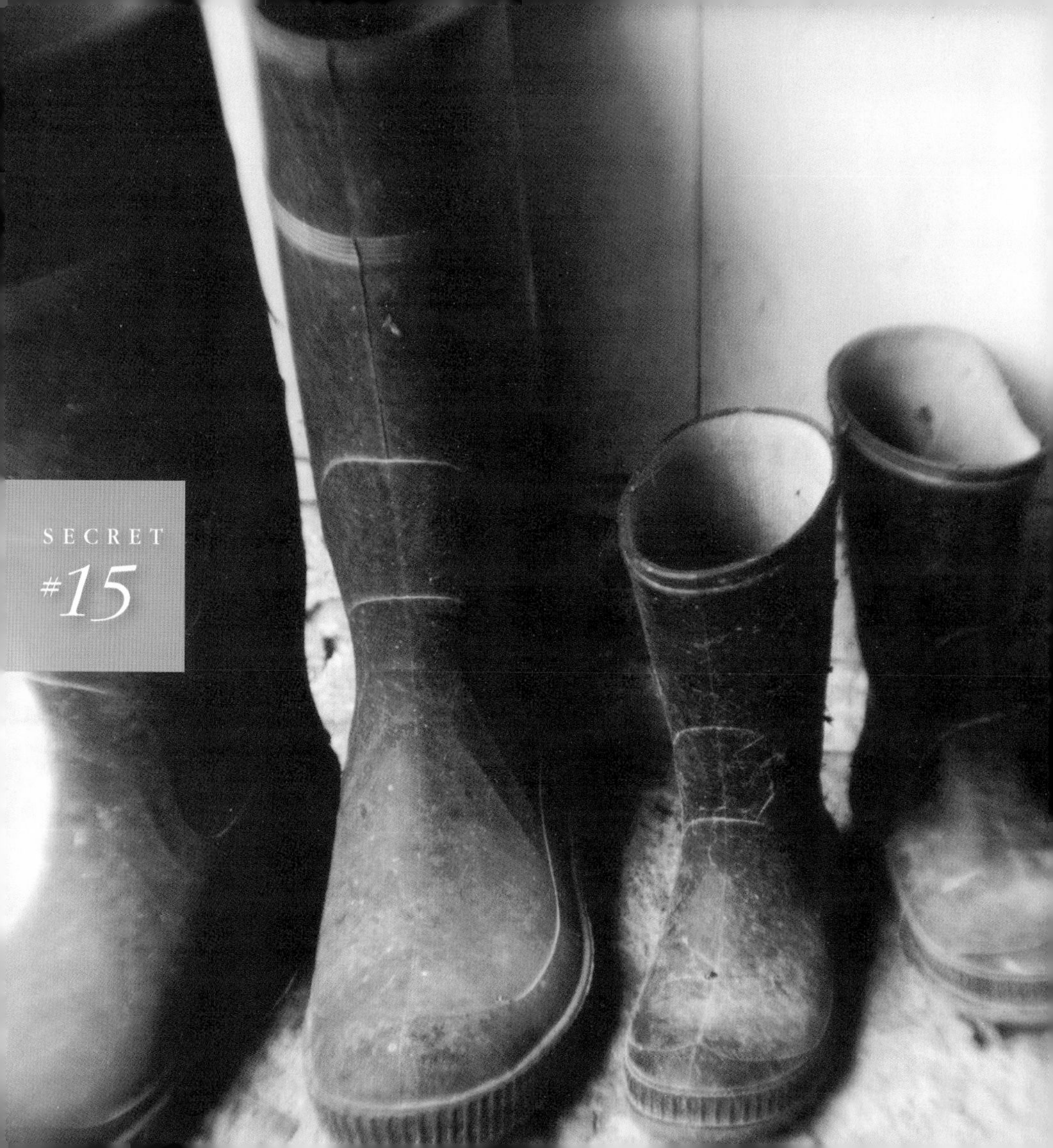
SECRET
#15

Tell me who admires
and loves you,
and I will tell you
who you are.

—*Antoine de Saint-Exupery*

Listen to the mustn'ts, child.
Listen to the don'ts.
Listen to the shouldn'ts,
the impossibles, the won'ts.

—*Shel Silverstein*

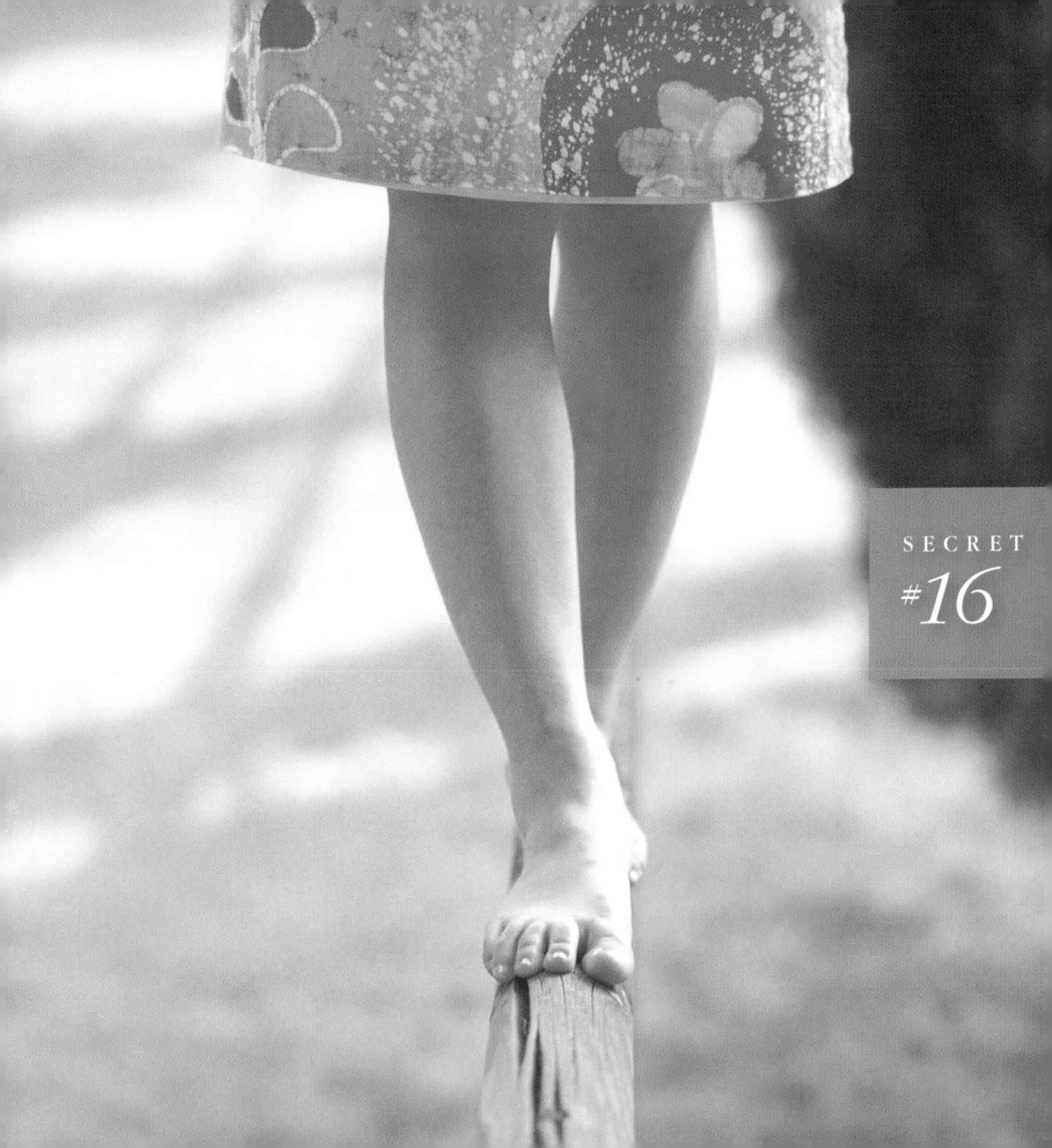

SECRET
#16

SECRET
#*17*

Hear the other side.

—*Saint Augustine*

Always forgive your enemies; nothing annoys them so much.

—*Oscar Wilde*

SECRET
*#18*

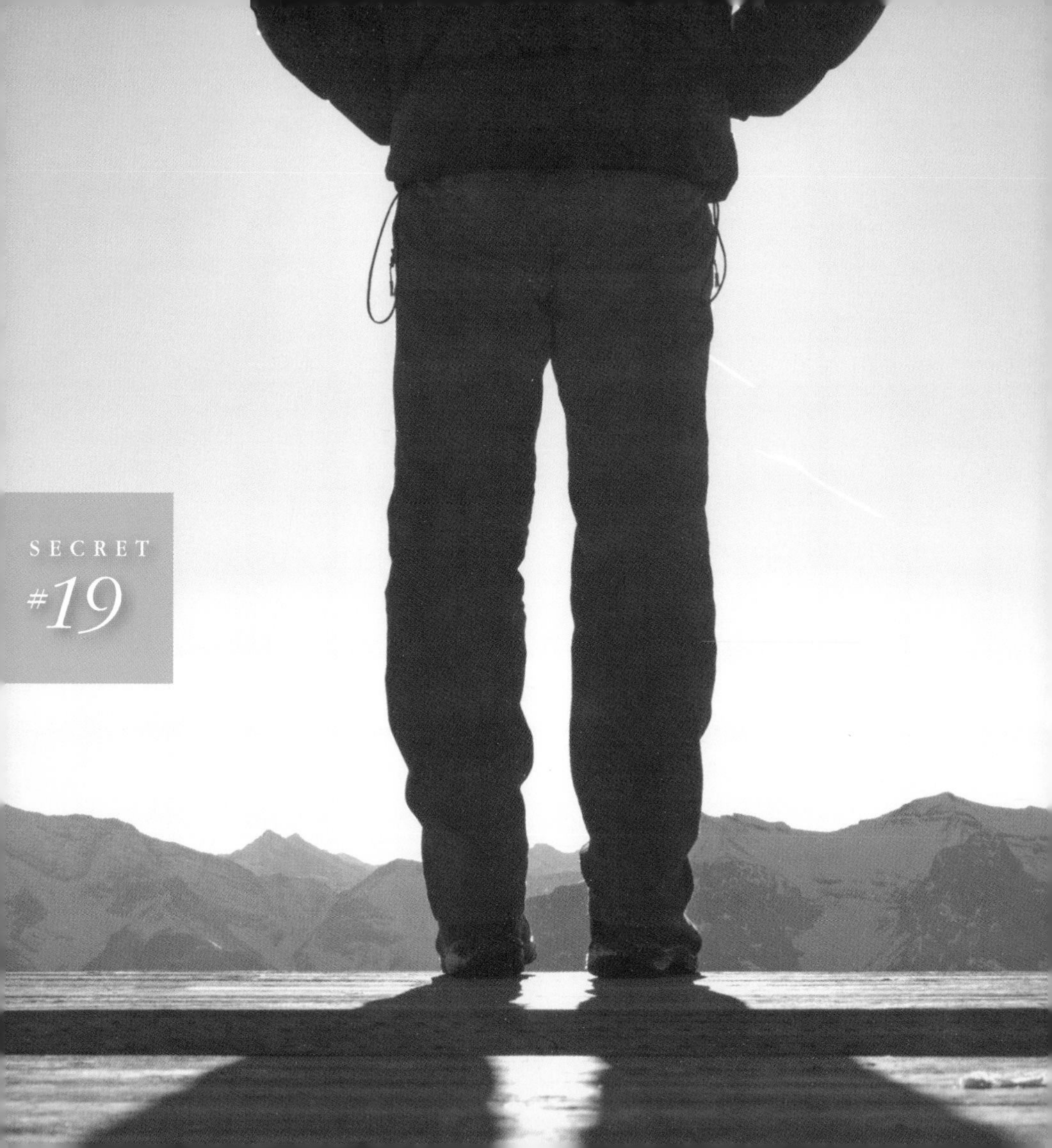

SECRET

#19

A man is a success if he gets up
in the morning and gets to bed
at night, and in between
he does what he wants to do.

—*Bob Dylan*

He is rich or poor
according to what he is,
not according to what he has.

—Henry Ward Beecher

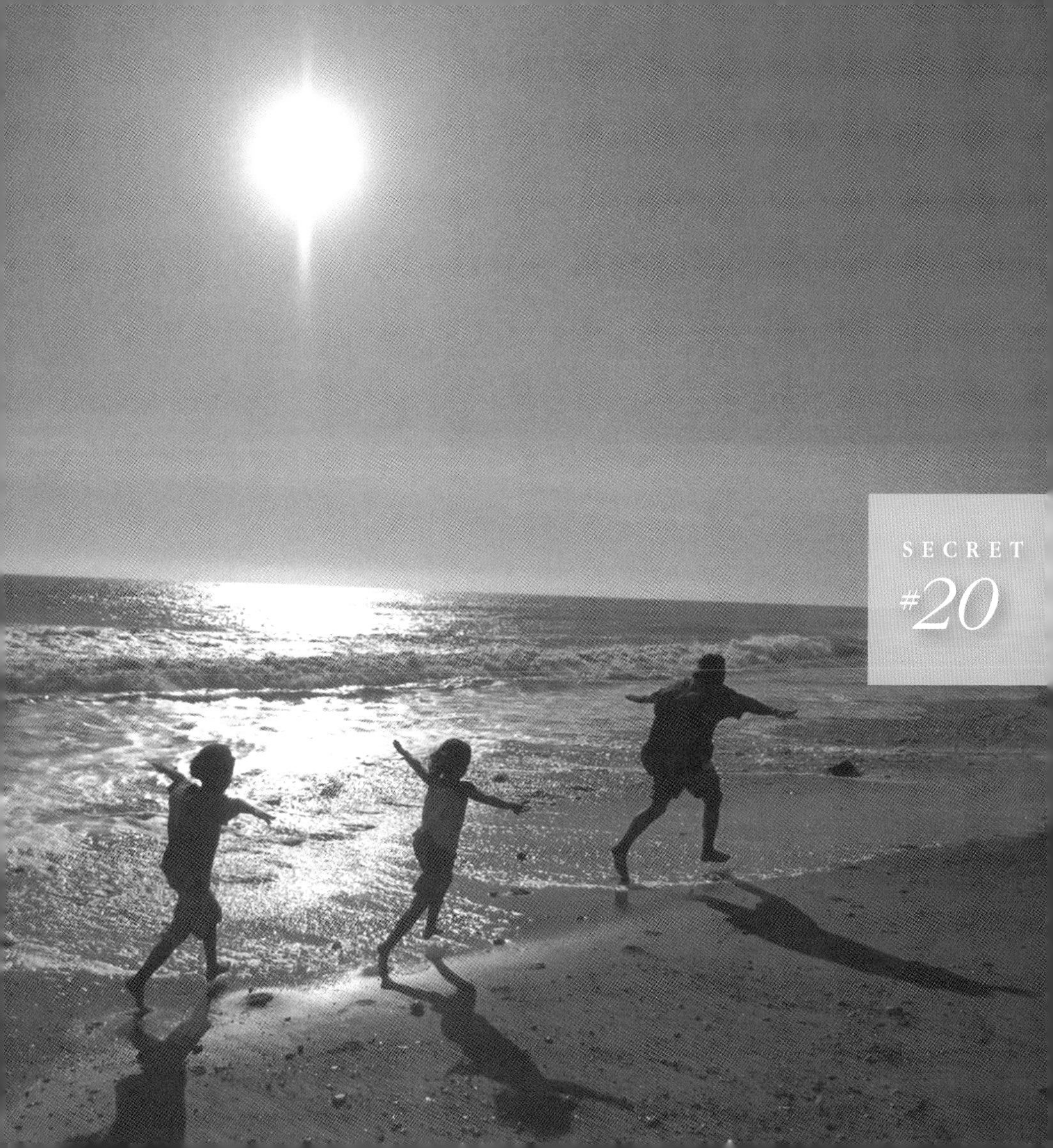

SECRET

#20

SECRET
#*21*

The foolish man
seeks happiness
in the distance,
the wise grows
it under his feet.

—*James Oppenheim*

There is
only one
happiness
in life,
to love and
be loved.

—*George Sand*

SECRET
#22

Laughter is
the shortest
distance
between
two people.

—*Victor Borge*

It is only possible
to live happily ever after
on a day-to-day basis.

—*Margaret Bonnano*

SECRET
#24

The cure for boredom is curiosity.
There is no cure for curiosity.

—*Ellen Parr*

Just living is not enough.
One must have sunshine,
freedom, and a little flower.

—Hans Christian Andersen

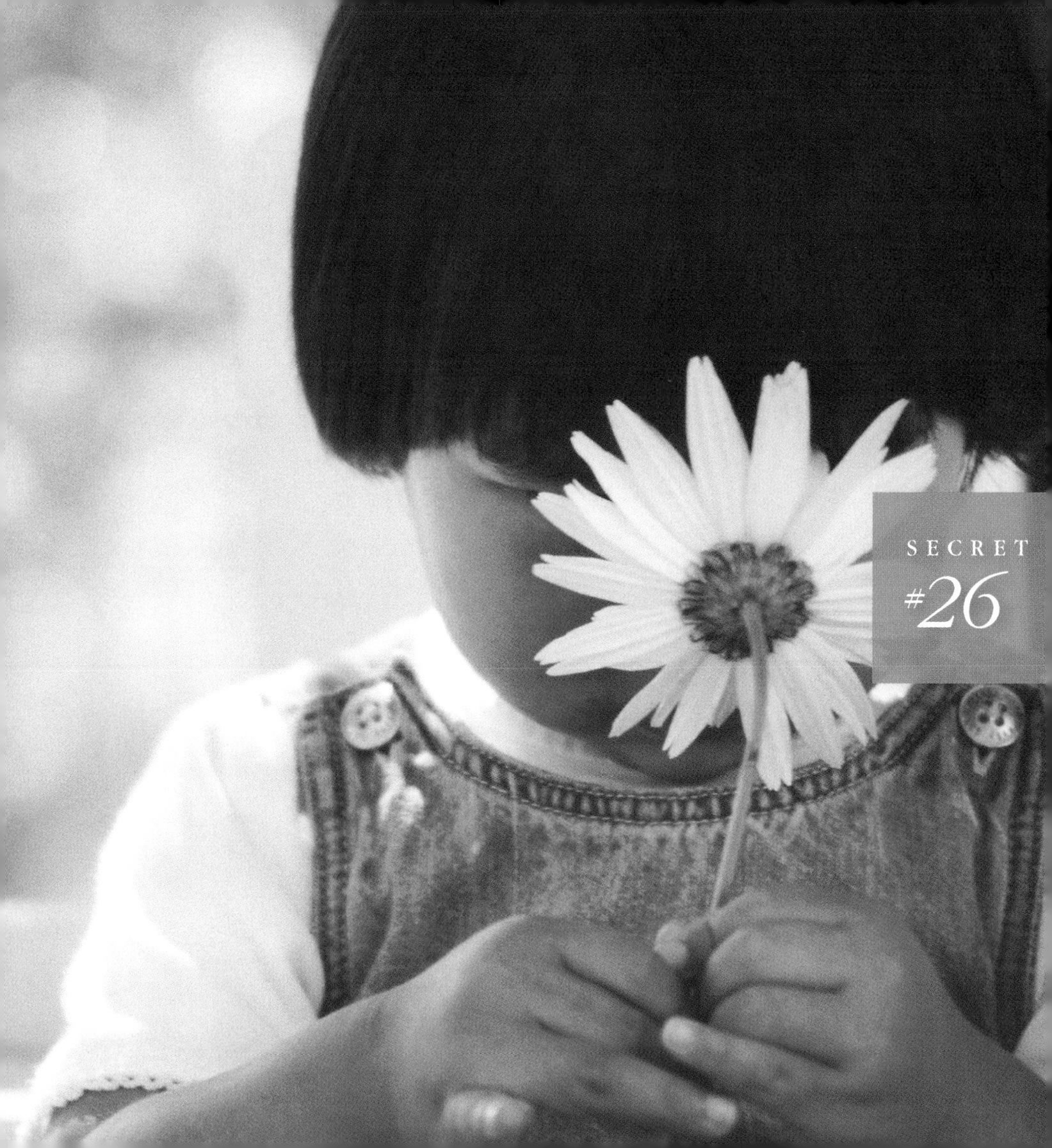

# SECRET #26

SECRET
#*27*

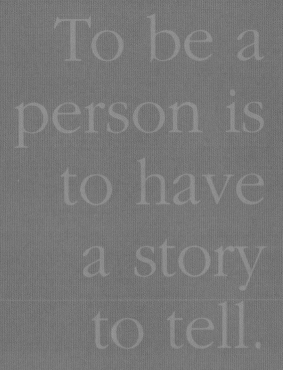

To be a
person is
to have
a story
to tell.

—Isak Dinesen

Be kind, for everyone you meet
is fighting a hard battle.

—*Plato*

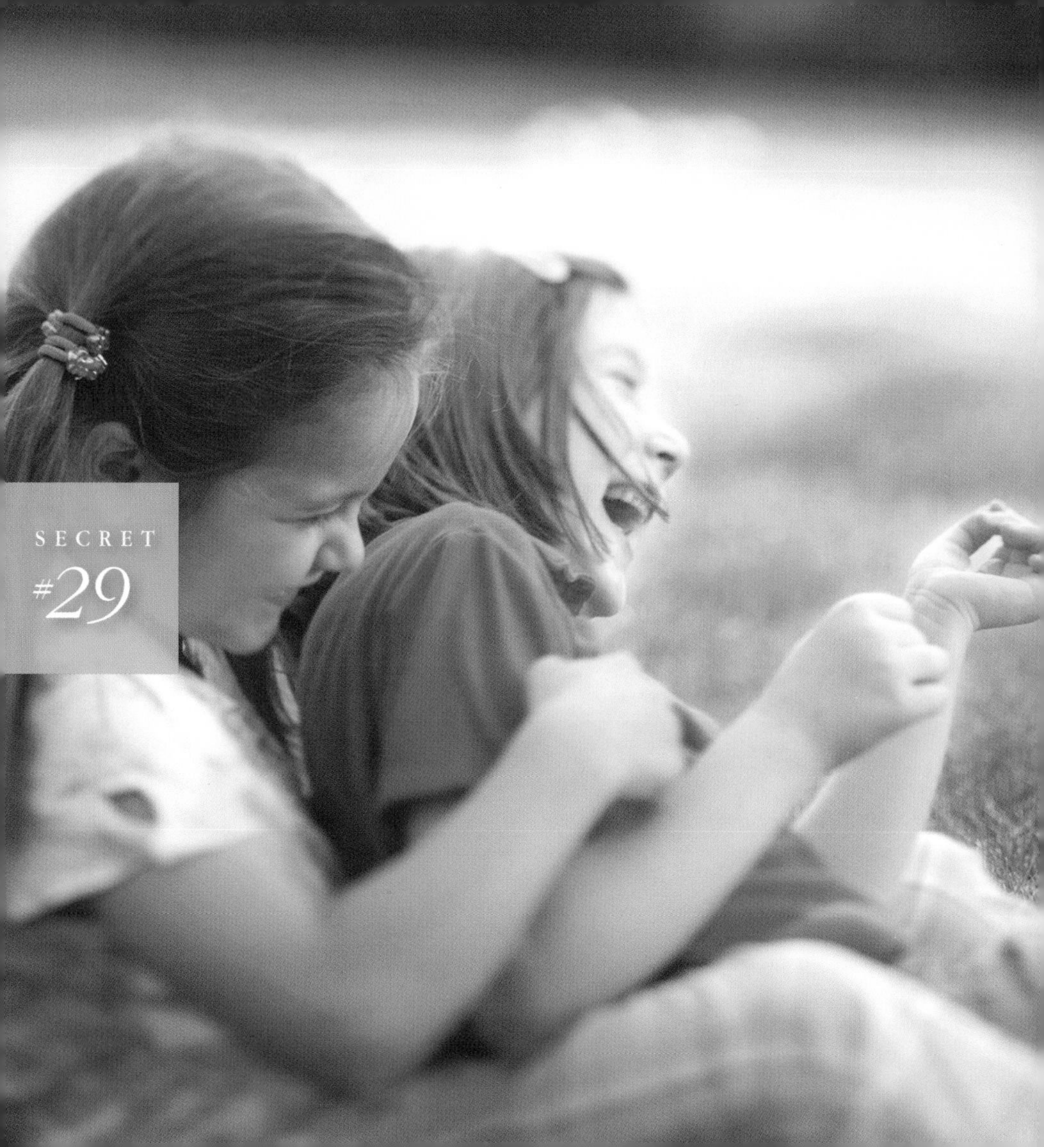

# SECRET #29

Be true to your work,
your word, and your friend.

—Henry David Thoreau

If indeed
you must be candid,
be candid beautifully.

—*Kahlil Gibran*

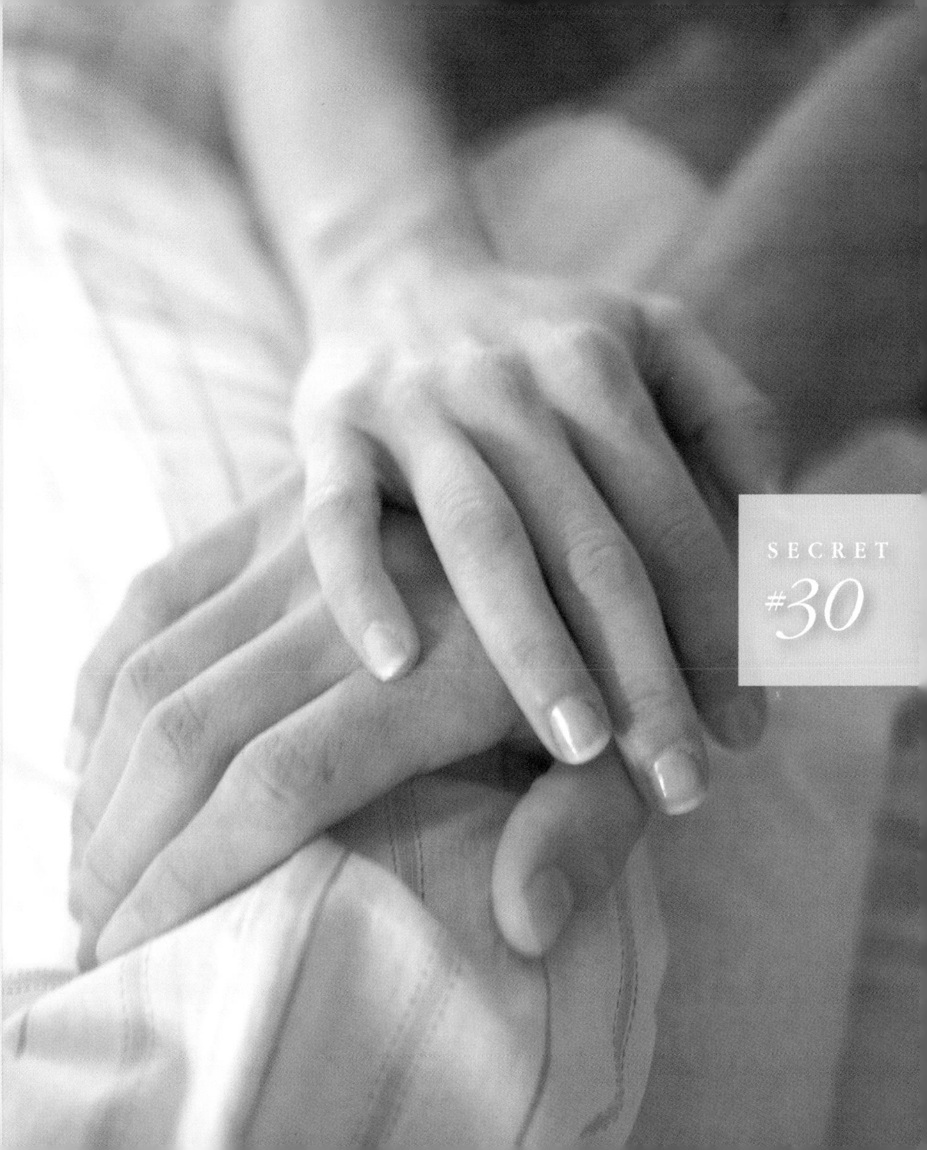

SECRET

#30

SECRET

*#31*

To thine
own self
be true.

—*William Shakespeare*

Whatever you are, be a good one.

—*Abraham Lincoln*

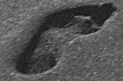

Have you enjoyed this book?

We would love to hear from you.

PLEASE SEND YOUR COMMENTS TO:

Hallmark Book Feedback

P.O. Box 419034

Mail Drop 215

Kansas City, Missouri 64141

OR E-MAIL US:

booknotes@hallmark.com